MW01244732

ORMUS

for the Soul

Select Poems

Fahredin Shehu

inner child press, ltd.

Credits

Author

Fahredin Shehu

Editor

hülya n. yılmaz, Ph.D.

Cover Art

Shuk Orani

Cover Design

William S. Peters Sr.
inner child press, ltd.

General Information

ORMUS
Fahredin Shehu

1st Edition: 2021

Publisher Information:
Inner Child Press International
www.innerchildpress.com

Copyright © 2021: Fahredin Shehu

ISBN-13:978-1-952081-48-4 (inner child press, ltd.)

$ 16.95

Disclaimer from the Editing Department

In order to maintain the poet's authentic voice, this publication has not undergone the full standard scrutiny of editing. Please take time to indulge this collection for the author's own creativity and aspirations to convey the uniqueness of his written art.

hülya n. yılmaz, Ph.D.
Director of Editing Services

Table of Contents

The Poetry

Petrichor   3

Table of Contents . . . *continued*

Aquamarine Clouds of Mystery 19

Table of Contents . . . *continued*

Table of Contents . . . *continued*

Epilogue   87

Foreword

There is no better passport to travel nowadays than with a book of poems. Through it, we get to know people and it allows us to travel all over the planet, regardless of any border. This is the case of *Ormus*, Fahredin Shehu's book.

> Every time and always,
> I recall the mossy ruins of my
> distant past where the soul
> wandered.
>
> On the aquamarine velvet notebook,
> a heavy Pen writes harshly
> with blood instead of ink and
> straight letters for the curved world.

His pages contain in their verses a universal message that allows us to know it in all its magnitude. These poems that you are going to read contain time, memory, nature and love, integrated into a pure and meaningful language.

> Dark forces wearing shinny accoutrements,
> blinding thus the easy goers and the poor
>
> I heard every move,
> each of them releasing a weeping sound
> between Knowledge, Destiny, Experience and
> slides of Life's occurrences

Ormus refers to the land of the poet, a land that bleeds and flourishes with a strong hopeful breath, not only for her but for a world that blurs in torment.

What may a poet do for
                        tomorrow
Other than guess the future
As a blind seer, thus,
To ridicule and mock himself
Of what the machine can't
Calculate and call it Love

Finally, the poet takes us on an inner, humanistic and existential journey, from which we return full, satisfied and with images to remember. But with a certain mandate, we too must do something. Hopefully in poetry.

Esteban Charpentier
Poet
Argentina

Preface

This poetry collection is a fractal of my augmented soul; therefore, I wanted to entangle my readers in its vibration to elevate them to another state of consciousness. The book is a representation of the power of the kind of word that even the most sophisticated artificial intelligence cannot reproduce. Nothing new was intended to showcase despite the reflection of vision, dream, and the untold truth that each and every one of us possesses as a hidden gem deep within ourselves.

Ormus is an extract of gold, the monoatomic particles of gold that I used in my meditations to enhance higher states of consciousness. In this case as an author, I wanted to endow this *Ormus for the Soul* to those who through Love attain the Divine.

There are two, so to say, train tracks that made possible the birth of this artistic book which emancipated to the level of Theurgy and objective art (something to experience in hush, serenity, solitude while being united with the universal reality of synchronicity and quantum reality). The first one was inspired by the following quote from Arthur Schonberg: "If it is art, it is not for all, and if it is for all, it is not art." As for the second path, it was shaped by my desire to create as genuine a book of poetry as I have not written before, and as something that cannot be reproduced in the future.

In *Ormus*, the reader has the opportunity to touch and tackle the most subtle partiture of the infrasonic music of the soul the frequencies of which shall vibrate from the outer to the kernel of Hesh ("Hesh" stands for androgynous, a joint male and female entity that is just like the Soul and Light in themselves).

All I wish here is to thank all whom I have encountered either virtually or in person, by the vibration of whom the invisible tapestry of creation took a visible form. My thanks also go to those who contributed either with their reviews, words of dedication, art work, editing and publishing in order for the reader to have a piece of our souls. *Ormus* is another tribute to humanity and an example that good deeds and togetherness may create a synergy and beautiful art in its full beauty.

Dedication

B.H. or Before Humanity

A poem by Tarık Günersel

Dedicated to Fahredin Shehu

B.H.

to Fahredin Shehu

a quiet evening
        new moon
                a friendly wind
can a little waterfall
             turn into Niagara
        and all the mountains and forests
                    of the planet
   here
          happening
the modest stream
           is becoming
                an ocean
                  as we look
      reflecting green branches
          embracing small mossy rocks
unpretentious freshness
      as if
      these were the times
             B.H.
           Before Humanity
witnessing
   the monthly visit of our good old neighbor
   a rebirth
      of
     not only Rahovec
        Kosovo
        Earth
          but Nature
        as a scattered whole
        with its dynamic tranquility
wondering breaths

are becoming

        rivers

the little waterfall

    is now poetry

        word free

       with a brand-new moon

    enjoying clarity

        flowing together

Tarık Günersel

Poet, playwright, actor and director who worked at Istanbul City Theater as a dramaturge. His works include *Breaths of Infinity* (*Sonsuzluk Solukları*, a mosaic of poems), *My 300th Birthday Speech* (short stories), and *Becoming* (*Oluşmak*, a collection of his aphorisms and various ideas from world wisdom). His plays include *Billennium*, *Nero and Agrippina*, *Sociology of Shit*, *Threat*, and *Virtually Yours*. He has written four libretti for the composer Selman Ada: *Ali Baba&40*, *Blue Dot*, *Forbidden Love*, and *Another Planet*. His translations into Turkish include works by Arthur Miller, Samuel Beckett, Vaclav Havel and Savyon Liebrecht. His presentation of World Poetry Day to PEN International in 1997 led to its adoption by UNESCO. Günersel is the former president of PEN Turkey Center, has served in the PEN International Board between 2010 and 2012 in Tokyo, and initiated the Earth Civilization Project with various intellectuals from around the world in 2013.

The Poetry

Ormus

Petrichor

Ormus

the Earth smell after the rain . . .
a splendid Petrichor brings
Eons back to life, to my life
brings a primordial vigor
for eternity and a day more

Fahredin Shehu

Just a Slide of the Past

Out of those petty memoires
the muslin of experiences
unfolded, fluttering on
the light wind one could
believe
is a zephyr that
brought
all aromas
of tiny linden
flowers from afar

It is as we all forgot
the bloodshed caused
by human
depositing suffering
preserving it
for another age

. . . and the day will come
for me to stand firm
while the dark wind couldn't
bring down my extremities of gold
I am sure you've heard the story
of immoral queen and
an immaculate who brought for
a man. A mercy for
the Mankind – confused men
among all . . .
and all we need is
awareness and let the singers
sing and get the praise

Aromas of the Past

Summer nights
and the full moon
on the balcony we enjoyed
herb tea and I can still
hear the knocking
of the metallic spoon
on the bottom of
the porcelain mug
mixing honey – stirring with the tea

A firefly landed
on my arm
the right arm with the thrilled
skin, goose bombs and erected hair

I didn't believe in omens
not even today I read
the dreams with the
vocabulary of Men

Beneath the balcony
huge terracotta amphorae kept
the decaying Iris tuberose
in their sixth year
one more year – one more Me
closing the glass lids above
amphorae and above them
pots of succulents

They were the days
they were the nights when
the life had the human meaning

Fahredin Shehu

Those Beautiful Seconds of the Past

He brought a handful
of Tonka beans for the base

She evaporated all liquids
from the petals of jasmine
and dried pistils of the saffron

I collected the dews early
in the morning,
observed and guessed
which star tonight shall
climb to the sky and
decorate it
darker than the ink it was
in those Times. With what shall I
blur tonight? With what shall I quench
my thirst for knowing
when the dews are dried and
the seconds are counted in vain?

Another Image of the Past

I have forgotten
the touch of wet, freshly-cut grass
and the thrill which runs
faster than a current
from the sole to the top of the head

In this urban desert,
we didn't cool our feet
like swans in the pond
but with the compressed
Nitrogen in our sneakers
with the perfect cushioning

This time, we shall braid
life differently;
so we may later see how
its curls create a texture
for another age

Fahredin Shehu

Mists of the Past

A huge mountain shaded
the emerald field with
dandelions like stars
in the sky all over

The work produces a sweet
essence – I got the bee
zooming in on my straight hair,
blown by the wind

Pearls of sweat in my forehead;
some of them dried, fell, blown,
taken afar from the eyesight
. . . and the river nearby,
gurgling, taking away
some light

They said to us: there were
the souls of drowned men,
now wandering in this
vast green field, covered
lightly with the mist

Aromatic Memories of the Past Age

The poppies
even they . . .
made it more beautiful
among the metallic sounds
of golden wheat leaves
on my most beloved July

Oh, at that very age . . .
I stood firm to expel
my inner demons, and
wrote the first verses
with the smell of earth
before it decomposed; bows,
twigs and leaves of ivy
sneaked inside the trunk of oak trees.
A splendid petrichor!

Down there . . . the ravine beyond
my eyesight transported
                    all my fears
some demoiselle with metallic
                    greenish turquoise bodies
silently copulating to extend
                    their lives through
their progenies in another season
long plus millennia they shall live
                    in peace, while we
the Human-grind souls
chop hearts and suck the blood of each other

Remnants of Another Eon

Turquoise ink, I save
to write only about love
and with the blood letters of a promise,
keeping it in the box made of
oak tree wood, copper leaves for its lid
and a splash of heavy lacquer above all
Moschus, sprinkled on my epitaph of Graphene,
light letters, inscribed
with green laser, state:
"herein floats the Soul
of a Light-man – a remnant
of another eon".

The Bottle of Age

Every time and always,
I recall mossy ruins of my
distant past where the soul
wandered.

. . . aghast by the torments and
ropy desires for the life
yet to become.

Lungs are filled with the odor
of oak moss, and time after time,
with the pine resin fragrance and
iodized air of the sea.

The breeze brought on that time
soul's nacre of my memories
and the gurgling whims of youth.

I pitied them as I do now all
traders who merchandised
their creed for the mustard seed.

Slowly, the bottle of age is getting
filled by the years I have
 to always remember and take
in to other dimensions.

. . . layered stripes of memory,
leaving behind the places on the brain,
like bruises turn to yellow.

Fahredin Shehu

The Wine Cellar

"Open those eyes given to you
and fuse with the universe
if you open only the mind's eyes
you will never see the love in full"

Conference of Birds by Attar
Translated by Sholeh Wolpe

. . . keeps centuries of labor
in Grapeland where many have
passed through as conquerors
as those who only wanted to marry
and as those who wanted
to drink the best wine only

in there through millennia,
microorganisms were multiplying
and none of us dared to count them
by number, none by their age

when I opened my eyes and fused
my glance with the luminous star,
undressing her devoré,
I could see her torso and
the fog unfurling from her body,
dispersing across the universe
a singularity in its vastness
spell bounded our vision
I could see none but us

Ormus

There was a cellar up there,
pouring that wine from turquoise
amphora – some said, it was ambrosia
that Illyrian sages extracted from
honey and served in the Delphi Oracle
some said, it was only water
that poured on us mercy, and in it,
the particles of Soul and the fractals
of the life that has yet to come

Fahredin Shehu

The Prayer Rug

With the power of another world,

I borrow the moment

where remembrance and longing

are spun like a silk thread

for a prayer rug.

The Velvet Notebook

On the aquamarine velvet notebook,

a heavy pen writes harshly

with blood instead of ink and

with straight letters for the twisted world

"V", the Sign

. . . and the flock of pilgrim birds flew
in the distant shores
on the way, marking the "V" sign
in the sky, aware of flight and bones,
full of air and wings of sin-sprinkled feathers

. . . talking the language of God, remembering
the words of God upon their very creation,
supporting each other, avoiding maladies
of what they left behind

. . . not turning back their heads with one aim
they hit the distance to the next exile
the aim of unification to set
in the next dwelling where prayers
are done utterly in vain,
and the longing as bitter morsel
is swallowed to cure
the past lives – far from bliss
for who knows how many will die
on the way toward the known
by the script inscribed in their genes?

A Crimson Pillar

On a crimson pillar of my pain
a demoiselle lands lightly.

Upon a silent shriek of heart's gate
of mine, she stands un- thrilled.

I pity . . . yet I pity those who see
the only friend, the one they see in the mirror
for life is no less than a miracle,
and all the rest is past or future.

Aquamarine Clouds of Mystery

Ormus

everything but a dream

non-dream, it wasn't

under the shade of a blood-color maple leaf

Inter-hearing

Between layers and epithelium,
dimensions have no limit
a belling echo is released
amidst canyons of memoires

My walk there
emits a serious spectrum,
visible as never before

We sat for a celestial meal
and an instant nap

The pain was precisely cutting us
a laser from the emerald head which
was extracted from arranged layers of granite

There in Antwerp Masters,
the diamond cutters pray
prior to commencing their work

We never pray the Moses prayer, Ta Ha 114
What kind of ignoramus we are!
There's no tongue knotted and those
unknotted from nine knots that
may say the grandeur and the volume

Political children were listening to shrieks
of their pain, their dirty toilets

People's malfeasants, merchants of their souls
were mocking the misfortune of others and their
fear, they were layering deep in their soul to take
away as their solely owned dowry

Ormus

Dark forces wearing shinny accoutrements,
blinding thus the easy goers and the poor

I heard every move,
each of them releasing a weeping sound
between Knowledge, Destiny, Experience and
slides of Life's occurrences

We observe and we feel bad,
we listen between pores of collective memories,
we march down the Abyss,
reckon the sinking and recall
Erica Jong's *Fear of Flying*

That which in the beginning was LOGOS.
It remained so

That which in the beginning was READ.
It remained so

I say HEARKEN!
Let it be so

Whereas we shall inter-hear
with the ears of our heart
for Eternity and
a Day more

Let the Human . . .

Let it be the last leaf
that is felt in early spring
in there, in here, in everywhere
when the blooming Acacia
intoxicates with the divine perfume,
that fragrance from the doorsteps
                        of Paradise's Gate,
filling chests and dazing hearts

Let the World stand today,
celebrating the same loftiness
of our Souls where colors
only enrich the bouquet
of Humanity and rejoice
its abundance, making jealous
all other creation – even those
manlike predators that see
no mercy in blood shedding
and bizarre exploitations

Let the Men nowadays
understand the difference
of Man and other Creation
is merely to realize how
beautiful it is to be a Human
and that it suffices
in its plentitude and diversity.

The Tapestry of Being

there are two things that
Man strives to understand:
Love and Poetry,
for they became
the show of the profane

on that very day,
when the men shall undress them
make them naked and hear
the cry of the Newborn,
the blast from the sky shall
blind the rest, and all clouds
shall restart

there are two things that
can reset time:
Love and Poetry,
for they became
the heavy slide that time
cannot drop to light
on that very day, the rest
shall see the moving images,
a dreamlike manifestation
they could hardly believe
until they melt in it and become
a part of it
for another eon

the blast from the heart shall
beam-blow the truth
in a time-based tapestry of being

Whom to Challenge

On the sky-wide dome,
clouds were forming the story
he tried to jump,
never competing with anyone

He himself was his own challenge
three times he competed
and exceeded himself
he himself was his to suffice
he himself was his counterpart,
and it remained so

Integration

Strange but real
sad but true
weird but still enduring
what comes next as the unknown
show of an irrational

Is this a sealed destiny
or a clay-like life that
I may craft with my Galatea and
erase the borders of distinction
and doubt whether it
is a Love-Life or a Life-Love entity
or both simultaneously happening,
leaving me to eternally ponder deeply
what it is or what it may be in my struggle
to make it US, for US is a total fulfillment
the integration to the ONE – The Real

. . . as it was in the beginning

They gave up all definitions,
layered fossils beneath the argument –
who's older? the hen or the egg

Massive droplets of rain
the soil as dry as talcum
release the petrichor we largely
enjoyed – the one we miss
massively today and more and more
in search of poetics and truth

Fahredin Shehu

The road we passed in vain . . .
if it goes out of our selves,
then nothing have we ever achieved

the World was not ready yet
to absorb a living human
even up between the heavy clouds
the breath is focused on the Constellation
of the heart. Some thousand nerves
from the brain of the heart
which the human named "Intuition"

We laugh upon every definition,
and still, none can order
a meal with algorithm
but solely by word
as it was
. . . in the beginning

Complainers

When organic and synthetic algorithms
merge as nail and flesh, and
when men shall choose
who's going to love the Absolute,
no other essence or aldehyde
shall perfume our souls
the complainers will love
heavy tears that hardly leak and
all sorts of balms and collagen
to heal their wounds,
neither shame nor pity
no other life form but
Life itself will bring solace
to the indifference once
proclaimed as holy

A Strange Kind of Bliss

Thinner than the air
today, I dwell in a higher
form of bioenergy – the light in
the front, the light behind
the light up, the light down
the light out, the light in
all smells of pleasure
enfolding his mortal flesh
all sounds of serenity
turned on with this cosmic sound
all fears disappear
all memories disappear
all tastes disappear
all wishes disappear, too
all I want is bliss

An Idyllic Winter Landscape

Parochial entities in
idyllic winter landscapes
tons of unheard melodies
spreading a skunk
up and down till
the highness of the white clouds

Whom to pity
whom to mercy beyond
                    the imaginable

Whom to lay down
the soul on the palm of hand without lines
no palm reader may define
the roadmap of perpetual ignorance

Fahredin Shehu

Older Than She Appeared

On that Thursday afternoon
heavy clouds merged with ice flakes
and the heavy rain was about to
blow away not only remnants but
the bows and un-ripe fruits
from the Peach tree
and the rest of the orchard

Even fences that hindered
rosters and hens of a neighbor
to cross the alley of veggies
she took care so ardently

Never did she know the dates but
counted days by eggs
and the mornings by the rooster alarm

She put four sieves on the four corners
of the house – an old belief to preserve her plants
from heavy hail

In her hair happiness and sorrow were braided
in her azure blue eyes was the image
in the fractals of the universe
in her heart – a cosmic singularity
in her walk – the graciousness
of a honey-faced fairy

. . . but on that Thursday afternoon
she feared the death of many;
not her own. No. Because she lived
in her tenth life of circular realization

31

The Theurgist of Words

Pealing pomegranate while
winter was approaching and
a handful of walnuts he gave me
to show how much he cared about
the one who wants to become a physician

Then the war started in Croatia and
he got back to learn swimming
in the ocean of the Eastern knowledge
said knowledge was as far from the wisdom as he was

He even abandoned drying the leaves
seeds, roots and distilling petals
and the pollen – using honey to heal
his body and the prayers to ease
his restless soul

While he continued to study still
from the Taoist pharmacopeia
a receptive dream became
a vision that appeared
out of every perception:
a building of a honeycomb shape
forty neon-white light entities surrounded
him, standing in the middle of a huge hall

A ten tons-heavy book, a written parchment
instead of paper – round letters he could
not read – a brass, emptied perfume bottle
in the middle of the giant book as if it
was embraced by the parchment

Fahredin Shehu

The perfume filled the vast hall and
a lighted white eye-blinding hand
touched his right shoulder
to wake him up – to awaken him
for some decades to come

. . . and he left his bed
the pillow wetted by sweat and
the mattress of Moschus smell was hard to remove

He opened a window
like a baboon, he stretched his palms
toward the morning sun
to absorb rays – to fill his spirit
with life and to realize he is
what he is – a theurgist of words

No Point

Ice chunks floating on the turmoil-sea
standing by a man full of sorrowful memories
when he was not alone

He wanted to roll a dice of
life and death, but with whom?

Perhaps with his whims and recollections
of the past days when the youthful
outbursts and the path were not
red with rose petals, thrown on the carpet
nor ever a thorn-filled
alley of despair

When even water was bitter and
the fragrant extremities of plants
stretched their bio-limbs to touch
the sun rays of the late fall

Chirping voices of the birds somehow
made him think he was experiencing
the last days on this planet of hate
where love had evaporated
its essence for long, plus more times
even a tornado wouldn't
surprise him now
so, for time and time again
if it is not said in vain:
"When no one and not a thing
are able to surprise you,
what's the point of living, and
despite all living, being without
The Beloved?"

The Remnants of the Day

The old saddler in front of
                    his workshop
braids the smoke of heavy tobacco
in a mildly hot summer day,
observing the passengers
with the cellphones and prolonged
noses over them – one may think they
are all Pinocchios – crafted
liars and deceivers

In an old city quarter, in this very
heart of the past occasions,
pigeons are flying over without fear
there are flies on the decayed
fruit remnants on the pavement,
thrown away by careless pupils
in their procession toward school

A siren of a maddened machine
warns – wakes up all
who stood there bewildered

Far from sight, much farther from the heart

We used to collect the licorice roots
never realized what she used them for
he was cooking in a huge dish
the maple to prepare syrup

Winter was approaching elegantly
we even felt it in our bones
guess what pain my grandmother felt?

Ormus

Our orchard was not so huge,
big enough to plant all kind of saplings
and other vegetables – sufficient for those
who don't demand a cent from a neighbor

We never knew what the war stood for,
apart from what we saw on TV
the Iran-Iraq war

Far from sight, much farther from the heart

She died while I was studying
while others barely shed a drop
of sweat to pass

Hard were those letters
triple as hard were the syntaxes and
the Trigon lexicography

Not Kabbalah – not the mystical science
of letters and numbers

A language of becoming, knowing
of the tenth reincarnation of suffering

Yet today, I am a silhouette and
gloomy – bitter dark than the darkest stone

Worry-less

The old vineyard was among the few
orchards my late father cultivated
as I strived for art by then

Mother rabbit left the nest
in search for the food. There – small rabbits
frightened by my shadow, they felt
I was still eating meat

July was hot – when the first batch
of grapes started to ripen. I collected
the grape leaves from the top of the twigs
for my Mom who used to preserve them
for winter days, to roll meatballs and
rice and spices for a decadent meal
in the frozen days of December

This can never be a bygone memory
alone the smell of a delicious dish today
resurrects all scenarios of the life
I used to live carelessly and worry-less

A Mere Passenger

Our small city still keeps in
                     its shoulders
all what our forefathers stood for
work, dignity, respect, bravery
craftsmanship, parchment folios
of genealogy from the times when
                     the Sun was adorned as god

She walked barefoot
on a stone bridge in a nearby town –
full of history

The fortress of old times was
observing and guarding the city from
the top of the hill

Down the hill, a place vendors used
to call "the devil's valley" . . .
they claimed to have seen fairies
flying in and out of the shrubs
until the devil appeared . . . and the evil
old ladies, all in white tunics,
laid down their long hair covering their faces
Pagans adorning the evil entity
on the night of St. George

One day glowered with honeysuckle
fragrance and that of Melissa and Lemongrass
I went to town and saw her in
her elemental splendor

Fahredin Shehu

Bewildered I was till delirium
upon my awakening – seven comets
braided their tails

The planets left their marks on my skin
to map the path
my path
and
the image of the Sagittarius constellation
imprinted on my forehead
so the Watchers can read
the hushed story of the earthly
life of a star walker,
a passenger of the Bridge

The Shine – the Shrine

*"The mind is not a master in
the art of love;
Love cannot labor in the brain"*

Conference of Birds by Feridüddin Attar
Translated by Sholeh Wolpe

Surrounded by the graves of Sufi masters
the main shrine
having preserved the times of remembrance
dispels the evil and offers shelter
to the travelers of all kinds

A spring beneath the shade
of a wine arbor – older than any other
known ones in the region,
some, aged four hundred years

She will cease to give shade and
fruit in the year when the enemy
kills the master while praying
and remembering
The God's Highest Name

Another shall replace her
Today, the replacement celebrated
twenty years – we do not adore it
but enjoy the transformable smell
of earth into lung-filling pollen
of tiny grape flowers

Fahredin Shehu

Yet we can labor Love
still
in our hearts

Ambrosia

A world between two ears
to some and heavy clouds
to others brings only the storm
and a vortex – below the throat,
down to the heart of a constellation
of Love – to the sublime numbers
that humans cannot explain
those Octonions that operate
in eight dimensions

What is human, for God's sake?
For all those years, those who believed
humans descended from Eve, who was a woman
who understood the language of snakes

For all those years and all those sages,
the humble and the strikingly arrogant
could not explain

. . . and the river of gold melted
the clouds of gold-dust,
making shade to the beloved
children, born out of love

In their ambrosias, they drunk
powered ORMUS to prolong life,
to awaken and to enlighten

Fahredin Shehu

In there, two Georges and the Jin
invented the misery

The yellows – thousands killed
in one hour, two blasts and

Georges and Jin called
them yellow ants – just to subdue them

This Dry-Day Age of Mine

They were classifying stones
to decorate the pavement,
a mosaic of life –
a mosaic for life and beyond

Friends called me to go
swimming in the river
far from home

Father was strict
I dared not to ask him permission
unless I lied to him as I was
going to shop a chain for my puppy,
a Yorkshire terrier
he brought from Vojvodina
some days ago

I didn't know how
to put those days in the memory ampules
to preserve them in a velvet box
all decorated in nacre and silver
and satin flushing red inside
emitting the oak moss and ambergris
and Tonka perfume of my Mom

In this dry-day age of mine,
smog and the stench of rotten
fruits suffocate and drown
us down to the ravine,
all blood and bones
of the past ages

Fahredin Shehu

Not Fewer Than Three Worlds

Sometimes, feelings
slipped through the soul
like beach sand
through the fingers,
later blown by the wind

The sun rays used to feed my cells,
giving potency to exhausted limbs
among bushes and briars
between stone plates, it woke up
a lizard that was dormant
in the season of the cold

They liked us
the snake guarded
the inherited treasure

Far at another site,
an urban part of the town . . .
the crowd quarrels for a morsel
and the malfeasant cries
for the loss of what he got not

We've never been bound
to the gold of the earth
even when
the stardust fell upon
our sanctuary – the roof was

Ormus

stable,
the basement kept us safe
bees safeguarded us from
                    negative vibes

It was as if I lived in two worlds
                    simultaneously,
it is not that I now live
                    in fewer than three

Some Prints

On that very day,
I got some message
it was not a call
not a letter to invite me
to the banquet of the Wise
neither was it the revelation
so I may delude myself and
proclaim to be a prophet
in an age that killed them all
it was, in fact, the call
to wake up from the men's lethargy
to wake up for another age
in which the alarm was not
a rooster any longer
not a handcrafted timer
made in some Swiss town

I stood with my pendulum;
it was the pen. Pencil and stylus
depend on the plain surface
I wrote those words
to love and print
for some years to come

The Poet's Lullaby

In an old archive, there are some
strange rules of lime-stoned parchments
in them the blood-letters with faded colors
are arranged to show a real palindrome
titles illuminated – all gold leaves

She unrolled the parchment
to show me my awe
she read my face, completely flabbergasted

It was a script from the pre-Babylonian times
none could read or decipher it so far
as for me, it was a map for another age
some new prophet of algorithms
could read and benefit
all I could do was to get
bewildered and lost in that image

. . . these label and price tags,
attached to the forehead

I could read, and could also see
with my naked eye
those crowns and scepters Men
used to hide zealously from
the eyes of the envious,
although my dioptric has doubled
    over the years

Those transparent beings
in expensive dresses and suits
who could guess their gender?

Fahredin Shehu

Those foods with gold leaves on top
to show prestige while in the other
fifth of the world hunger and war
devastated all, turning them
into ashes. What could a poet do?
Praise a tyrant in order to survive
or salute ministers of ill-doing
and highlight their worst faculties?
Burn all scripts and escape life
when life was only a sequence
while he was in love?

After the war took everything and
the windblown remnants,
roots and the twigs of plants
and
bones, veins and extremities
of animals in remote parts
of the planet – to somehow hide,
to somehow protect us from fear . . .
what may a poet do today,
instead of mourning
and lamenting for the age
that was human
that was full of belief
that was with God? And
what may a poet do for
                    tomorrow

other than guess the future
as a blind seer, thus
ridicule and mock himself
or what the machine cannot

calculate and call it Love;
other than love despite being
ignored, or better yet,
tortured, or in the worst cases,
tormented in-between two worlds,
in-between two ages that were never his . . .?
One day, when the poet realizes
he shall hold the key of the gate –
          that gate with the silent shriek,
passing it in a hush
like the walk of a cat on an old rug

. . . and the gate will open and
show two directions:
one that leads to Love
and
another
that leads to death

Careless as the most careless
one could be,
                he shall walk
on a golden macadam and feel
the coldness of the precious metal
early in the mornings of another world,
                    soaked in dew

The poet shall sing and put to sleep
all restless souls and he shall, too,
laugh madly together with the existence
he left behind – together with the life
he dropped like
            a peach kernel

Fahredin Shehu

behind his shoulders and never . . .
never turned his head to look at it – not out of fear
that he could become a salt-stone
but
aghast at humans,
aghast at human life
he used to live ardently

Sweltering Heat, Rain and Restlessness

With the tongues we tried
to catch the water molecules from
the dry air – camels, we were not
in those days, our skin became
dark and scaly – fish, we were not!

The first huge raindrop I mentioned
fell between the soil furrows
as open as baby graves
that corrugate our entire being

Whom to pity first and
whom to forgive?

As of my silence –
a long long long serenity
the hearing increased by its magnitude

 I could listen to the blood in my veins
and the liquid running
up and down my spine
the current produced in Mitochondria,
charging my molecules
and giving birth to love

. . . and Love is the sole faculty
my soul possesses,

Fahredin Shehu

regardless – if she's being sprinkled
with the most expensive Ambergris and
                              Oudh or
simply
by the priceless Divine Petrichor – the breeze
brought from a distance,
from the lands unpolluted
        by hatred

Ribbons

A black ribbon on the neck
of the tortoise is the mark that
one day they paid a tribute
to love – they scarified their lives
and sung the song of life

The red ribbon beneath
the skin of my throat
is the mark that once upon a day
I paid a tribute to love, too
I sacrificed my being and
sung a lullaby to a poet

. . . to the one that was unable to mark
his Art on his forehead and
seal his destiny

The Rosary

. . . made from lava stones,
made from amber, and some,
from the sapphire-blue as her eyes

In my bygones, she entered the room
the wings visible only by the eyes
of the one intoxicated in Beauty
that once it was the Jewel in the Crown
of Eternity – with a smile that shook
the pillars of the heavenly abode, and
as dense as the loftiness of Oxygen,
made it a blue lump of curiosity

. . . with the walk
the graciousness of which
bewitched all my "I's" – so they
assemble in that Temple where
infrasonic prayers, offers
                    and sermons
zoom like horrified bees
the labor of which produces
                a sweet essence
with the rosary – huge pearls
of which I now count the blessings
to live among Humans permanently

. . . while MEN sell even
their souls for a lump of happiness –
that is a grain of sorrow
and
the dew of curse

To Name a Misery

I wanted to give another name
to the Art which is difficult,
the one that to be and to the malady
that bears no name

I wanted to give misery
another name but feared
it might deceive the innocent
who may perceive it as bewilderment

I wanted to give another name
to love which is difficult to maintain
and to a longing that drains
the 'morrow from the aged bones of mine

The Difference

Empty shelves in our hearts
emptied by the most merciless of Men
that only resembled the Sapiens
who forgot through millennia
to find a pot and fill it with mercy

To remind those without a spark
of Truth and without that
what we treasure down and below
the visible, twinkling, and
pulsating wealth of spirit

Every time they look at nature,
they don't see an endowment

Every time we dwell in nature,
we unite with every particle
of her touching the erotic zones, and
distill the beauty through
her majesty – depollute
what the careless left as corpses
of their siblings they hated the most

Bird Shades

Shades of birds flying over our heads
they shall die one day – we shall die,
too, but life has to say something
very important; in a hush, it said:
from the day when stones and waters
heard our first cry – chasing love
from afar – out of body that emanates
old and new currents,
instead
of delivering it from within and
radiating until it burns the feathers
of the crows that brought misfortune

The ill-doing of those birds was
Unintentional – a program of their
Bio-algorithm. But the malady
is ours to handle as a widow
bears her covered pain deep inside,
yet she smiles at every birth

Fahredin Shehu

Searching for the Man

I could not find a grain of pity
nor a pint of fraternity when . . .
when calamity felt upon Men

Those who mocked my good-doing
and those who laughed upon
my fear – now, they are searching for serenity
in a world of turmoil where Time braids
its epochs with the ashes and
the dusts of civilizations

There's no Peace – stop pretending
the human benevolence when
none can sacrifice even a particle
of Goodness, kept hidden
deep in their DNA

Not even a lump of smell, kept
folded under the armpit

No feathers with tiny bells,
no praise songs for the kings,
no laments for the dead children

I still am . . . longing to meet a MAN
that is speechless yet he radiates beauty
and
splendor of heavenly bliss
in its divine reflection – if there ever
was such . . .
he must have ascended
to the Love-dimension of no return

It Is Felt

. . . in those moments
in those moments
far away from nowadays

in this moment
in this moment
far away from my Now-ness
there's a dew reflecting
my image
and
a spark of light
that opens the paths
of belief in
another time
in another place
that is closer
to the visible

so close that
it becomes invisible
it is felt
instead

The Morass

I am Wisdom in a transparent pot
and Imago on top of Metamorphosis

Water that decays across time
a spoiled milk in brain's capillary

A window shall refresh the end
a storm shall throw all the frogs
to the ceilings of old castles

From the river, learn the current
let these lumps of gold
                        surface above the water

When the time comes,
gold hunters will come along
to saturate their lust

The Protein War

Fallen feathers of the fallen fallacy
a man who drunk from the test tube
a mind that is confused
at a crossroad of existence

Between today's richness and
tomorrow's hopeful abundance

Transformers of borrowed energy

The sky is vast within

A protein combination in
a cosmic, walking creature
called the Body

The science shan't overpass morality

In order to fly,
a bird needs to fall
off its feather wings and
fail in the balance

We need more love
and empathy
and wisdom
and . . .

Shall we abandon these?

We are doomed to be
replaced by machines
in seclusion

Fahredin Shehu

I stand firm
and
tranquil
not by choice.
No!

I am here
I wait to reveal
who is human
and who
only resembles a human

For who knows
who conquered
the soul
and
who flies above . . .
darkly above
the contaminated soil
where a mixed swamp of blood
and
bile created
little ponds
all over

The 25th Hour of the Day

The veil of past times collapsed and
the mask of deception faded
another boy laments the death of the Mother
he mourns the sharp claws of his ill-fate
that mercilessly chops his flesh – immature and
immaculate before sin.

He'll grow up when the winds of seasons
will blow and throw him from Nadir to the Horizon
on the sea of life; no compass may orient him toward
the Ocean of Love he never tasted the waters of.

Long plus time, he'll embrace his stellar Souls
dispersed throughout ether and
find his solace at the 25th hour of the day

Fahredin Shehu

An Image of our Winterreise*

She brought the Christmas Stollen
few days after the New Year of 2006

Days were still bitter
the smell of war and spoiled bread
evaporation stunned our stomach

On the land of spilled-out blood
they told us . . . only poppies
break the monotonous tone of golden-leaf fields

In our laments medley with the sound
of barley leaves
metallic or crystalline echoes
nobody was able to discern

We took her to the cemetery
as miserable as Turkish tombs

She started crying
braiding her memory-pain
with the vision of the child's death

She survived her holocaust
She never survived her suffering
She never survived her fear

*Winterreise is German for "Winter's Journey", the famous
Franz Schubert Opus 89 which was based on 24 poems by
Wilhelm Mueller of Prussia and published in 1828.

Three Fives by Nine

I.

1. You said: "Be!" and it became six times
2. the repetition of a foreign genetic code.
3. The red dice, I throw in the Sea of Galilee.
4. I saw the senile while drinking the last absolute of life.
5. Nard, Amber, Jasmine, Cedar, Horse skin.
6. I also made an elixir of aromas – to wait
7. thus, that multiple wing light
8. to transport me below the Arctic
9. and from there, to the tears that I alone must smell.

II.

1. We tried to get drunk by dews, and by drunkenness,
2. our wine turned blood until we got sick and
3. searched for the diluted ecstasy. We remained intoxicated
4. as those in love in the eyes of whom only the star
5. distance is visible, while cheeks are wet by tears and turn
6. to nacre. Here we are, oh you Giants of Soul,
7. God's servants. Not like us, not like anyone else, but like you
8. The white light, while it enfolds you, while it covers
9. your rainbow-color luminosity.

Fahredin Shehu

III.

1. I saw them crying and crying I felt
2. in suspicion, I shall preserve this
3. stream of love for all
4. worlds in order to keep the freshness like
5. dew drops when they moisten bending
6. grass-leaves; doves observing and
7. butterflies with fluttering wings only
8. temporarily showing their beauty so to
9. leave their vestige, like poets leave their verses.

They Call It Perfume

Seven thousand petals of the white rose
hundreds of tiny Maghrebian
Jasmine flowers
some Tonka beans and Civet
some Soul particles, too,
and Ormus to fixate
the splendor of Life's joy

In my humility lays
a fractal of existence

In my humbleness – an echo
of the dimension of the Grandeur

This Word penetrates deeply,
tickling the hidden
and
dormant cells of loftiness

Fahredin Shehu

The Lament of Earth

How fervently you've preserved
the foreign narratives
you've adopted them
to sell them later like a fog of all colors

Even today, there are others –
sufficient to compete as who shall more and
who shall better keep the foreign past, and
there are others who strive to break
every membrane
to create new bio-algorithms
to uplift the life to another plane
to another dimension

Yet there will be Men
that will observe the World
here, with borrowed eyes
they will fold new images
in layers just like the fog thickens up
in this sky with a sole Sun

. . . and those who still want
to degust fresh wine and
dry artisan cheese, petals of May's roses
as a refreshment drink and a jam

When one day the exodus occurs
will Earth's colonies remember the homeland
they left behind, or will they like a snake
that shed its skin, never turn their head back?

Ormus

Go, experience the emptiness you've created, but
go aiming the return because
this Mother again shall await you open-armed,
shall long for some plus time,
accompanied with the sounds of Cello, Santoor, Piano
and the chirping voices of birds
with the wings of all rainbow colors

When in your recesses you hold your child,
tell them that somebody here knew your repentance
tell them a bit about the greed that you took away
like the dowry which will fly above
the weight-less Souls of yours
and that you've measured everything
with the human scale;

tell them about the Dice of Life and Death
. . . and the Death that defiled bearing a heavy shadow
wearing a black brocade gown, spreading fear all over;

tell them about the World with two Suns and
with the pointing finger toward Earth – toward Me,
this blue dew of Mercy that buries every evil in her chest;

tell them about the stars you've counted
while in your fingers calluses appeared;

tell them about the balloons of snivel from your noses
while playing with the sweat drops, ran down the neck;

tell them about wasps buzzing in your curly hair and
about the pond where swans were playing
while a blue metallic color demoiselle mingled among
cattails;

Fahredin Shehu

tell them about Love you've tasted
but never succeeded to understand;

tell
. . . about death, for God's sake,

the death of your most beloved and
the pain it caused;

tell them at the end about the Separation and
 the wounds it incurred.

Go, try the emptiness you've created solely
but go with the aim of a return because
this Mother shall again wait openheartedly,
shall long for some plus time
under the shade of the wild Chestnut Tree
while bees collect the nectar
for some other life.

An Emerald Knoll

On an emerald knoll, I climbed
full of breath
full of self

Under the heavy-cold shadow
of an Ash-tree, I took
a rest for a while
a chrysoprase-epitaph
was observing me appallingly,
crossly and somberly, and it said:

"You who in the world realized
that there is no East and there is no West
since your world is round;

You who said:
so, melt in Love
for eternity and a day more;

You who discovered the secret in the light
while in grey nights Moon-walkers
prayed to God:
See, that Then-ness and this Now-ness
are condensing with their naked bodies
in a solely single being while you still
recall when Time was a God."

The Evocation of Beauteousness

Black is not a color
as I absorb all beauty
of the Universe

White is not a color, either
as it erases all evil
by the brilliant shine of its face
soaked in all color

The Beauty emanates from the
Talismanic Temple of Greatness

Glory be to the one who ascends
to Divine Loftiness

With the kindling of His Light
which today I summon
the Possessor of the Greatest Light
will ease and lessen
the pain we all go through

. . . and the day shall come
for the dawn and dusk to have
a proper time – distance

From Him we sat
The hearing
The seeing

To hear the gurgling river
To see the falling colors from
the rainbow

Ormus

To collect the dews from
wet grass leaves

To hear the metallic gold sound
from the ripe wheat

To see the foamy fruit pulps
chewed by the mouths
of sweaty foreheads of
hyperactive children

To hear the Dolphins
while they copulate beneath
the deep Sea

To see peptides arranging themselves
deep in our chromosomes

To hear the flushing of electricity
in our Mitochondria

To cry while celebrating
Humanity

Truly, this is not Poetry
truly, I have condensed my soul
in the Beauteousness of Certitude,
for this is indeed a pact
so . . .
make it appear!
Quick!
Quick!
Hurry!
Hurry!

Fahredin Shehu

Right now!
Right now!

. . . a union of Man with Men
a Union of Men with The All
what is visible,
semi-visible,
and
invisible

. . . a Union of Men with
the heard, the somewhat heard and
the un-heard

for He sees us all
for He hears us all
what we crave inside
and
what we display
as a façade

for He is The Hearing
for He is The Seeing

Glory be to The One
The
One
O
N
E

How Could I Not Fall in Love?

It is us
who witness Evil
throughout millennia,
we are told that
the World was bleeding
yesterday
today
and
always
. . . but then the prophets were killed
and their most ardent proponents butchered

Today, they chopped off the spirit
from the heart of Poetry
and Faith entirely rooted off from Literature
The body of morality became weakened,
almost everything from the past was
questioned

It seems we'll never learn
to live decently and how to
grow – not to compete with other
intelligences but to at least
cope with them, and why not
fall in Love?

Fahredin Shehu

Luminous Alloys with No Name

Shall one day biochemical algorithms
safeguard our worlds, we will not
grow any expectations

The real wisdom lies in light
the secret is hidden in there

If the price of truth is in death
and the keys of the prophecy gate
are kept secret in tenfold boxes,
made of brass or other
luminous unnamed alloys . . .

then all what remains to be discovered
in the future cycles of evolution
shall be visible as a strip
of slides and pulsating lasers
in the vast dark recesses of the Unnamed
Dimensions that we are here, there, then,
now, previously, afterwards, all at once
manifested, manifesting manifestations
of Love that sees no color

A Separate Memory of the Heart

What is a poem, for God's sake
if it does not emanate from
the 40, 000 nerves of the heart,
beamed directly to the bi-colored
brain substance that pulsates
simultaneously?

The waves of mystery down to the heart
his/her pure heart that
illuminates all cells
and tissues
all flesh formations
and the bones
and the skeleton . . .

Fahredin Shehu

Talismanic Devices for the AI Age

we came down the valley
following the line

river descended from
the chest of the mountain

the sages left talismanic devices
for the benefit of all

keeping that memory
in the eyes of the children,
we saw the Divine presence
dews of the sweat in their forehead
testified our existence

in their ankle-bruises
we saw how
to undergo pain
we heard the buzzing
of wasps
in their curly hairs

oh, so beautiful
this world shows
all its abundance
to live,
and
to live
we remain

The Wedding of Intelligencies

that was our last entanglement
in a wheat-field with heavy cobs
like the wise man walks modestly
in the same street he encounters
three times the same awe-struck faces

we experience our double exposition
quantic is our love in essence

pain, sorrow, sobriety and spleen
all bridal like multicolor strings

upon our laugh, all the difference
disappears – all heavy tears
have melted and leaked from
hot, blushed cheeks. The wedding
of intelligencies
occurred silently
the dowry was our breath and
our blood that turned crimson
serenity has it saying:
"Deeper the Silence,
Shallower the Hearing"

Fahredin Shehu

I Am Still Longing
(on Father's Day)

Every day, I was longing
for a rest on his lap
and for a kiss in my forehead
after reciting the nighttime prayers

Every now and then, I long for
what I missed in my childhood
I can just now realize he couldn't
no, I couldn't

Because

He took care of his orphan brother
a bit older than us

He couldn't let him miss
Miss even a cent
. . . a lap,
a moment of happiness
the emptiness
grandpa left behind

Mom was always strong and
she remained so

Throughout the winds of life,
she stood firm

Strong, like faith
that holds the pillars of heaven

Ormus

Of a heart firmer than a diamond
she was

So many tears I saw in her face
yet so much love she gave
to us
to them
to everyone
to life

Fahredin Shehu

One Day

When the sky re-acquires its blueness
and the Ozone drops down the clouds
to wash our wounds

I shall wait men to deliver
their last sermon
or
a farewell speech

One day, I may sing since
I know the song but my voice
fails to hit the last octave
despite that I shall continue
the tweet will follow
and
neutralize my hissing and chirping

On that day, we shall observe
mists of perfume forming
the beauty and pleasure
equal to none

On that day, in the light
I shall dwell

The Ignored Sermon of the Parrot

they started to count
tiny little happinesses,
assembling them as beads
in a silken thread for a rosary
to chant again and again
over and over – the names,
they created themselves

it is as bricks are layered
in my biochemistry that
hinders the heavy
winds of time that blows
to ashes whatever appears
in front of it and
blows away far beyond
the eyesight

they used to forget the malice
and all the darkness it brought
forward and enfolded and
enveloped them tightly,
squeezing their limbs and eyes,
about to explode, losing
direction of observance

there is a feast outside for
all man-like yet the Man
was humble, reckoning
the development of this

Fahredin Shehu

manifestation, looking
for the kernel of the kernel
there in the light, where mystery
is hidden

vision is blinded
and
the mind is confused

Ormus

Epilogue

Photo Credit: Rromir Imami, Skopje, Macedonia, 2018

About the Author

Born in 1972 in Rahovec – South-East of Kosova, Fahredin Shehu graduated from Prishtina University with a degree in Oriental Studies. Passionate about calligraphy, he actively works on discovering new mediums and techniques for this specific form of plastic art. The author is Director of the Balkan Literature division of the Kosovo PEN Center, the director of the Kosova International Poetry Festival, founder of South European Literature Association in Sofia, Bulgaria and founder of Fund for Cultural Education and Heritage in Kosovo. Shehu is a writer, a critic, a seasoned independent scholar in the fields of World Spiritual Heritage and Sacral Esthetics, and a certified professional in adult learning on the platforms of Capacity Building, Training, Coaching, Mentoring and Facilitating.

Shehu has authored several books in Albanian, Serbian and English, which include *HERENOW* (2019), *Neon Child* (2018), *Elisir* (2017), *Bonds* (2016), *Maelstrom. The Four Scrolls of an Illyrian Sage* (2014), *The Pen* (2013), *The Honeycomb* (2013), *Pleroma's Dew* (2012), *Crystalline Echoes* (2011), and *Dismantling Hate* (2010). *Elisir* is a critically acclaimed work that was published in Italy with the title *Elixir* in its bilingual edition – in

Albanian and Italian. For *Bonds*, the author was nominated for the 2018 Pulitzer Prize for Letters. *Maelstrom. The Four Scrolls of an Illyrian Sage* is an epic poem in English in which Shehu offers spiritual insights, visions – a creative turmoil in mental faculties of the creator that oscillates between Theurgy and Revelation. This work displays a spatial-temporal efficiency of poetry as the best tool for telling the untold. *The Honeycomb* is structured through eight angels in eight human occupations as an accomplishment of Bee Honeycomb. The reader is then made into the ninth angel in a symbolism of Enneagram, an approach that is the first in Albanian.

Fahredin Shehu's literary creations have been translated into numerous languages, including English, German, French, Italian, Spanish, Polish, Greek, Serbian, Croatian, Bosnian, Macedonian, Bulgarian, Romanian, Swedish, Turkish, Mongolian, Arabic, Hebrew, Chinese, Maltese, Bahasa, Malaysian, Bengali, Frisian, and Sicilian.

As his following editorial contributions demonstrate, the author is an accomplished editor as well: The Anthology of Kosovo Contemporary Poetry in Turkish, The Balkan Anthology, an anthology on the paintings of Hieronymus Bosch and Pieter Bruegel, an anthology of poems by W. H. Auden, William Carlos Williams, Sylvia Plath, Anne Sexton, Czeslaw Milosz, John Berryman,

Billy Collins, Charles Simic, et al., together with the newly-minted poems, written especially for this collection, by Rae Armantrout, Peg Boyers, Robert Fanning, Alfred Corn, Ravi Shankar, Kaveh Akbar, Kimiko Hahn, et al. – with an introduction by the noted art historian Margaret A. Sullivan and her poet son, David Allen Sullivan.

For his role in bridging nations, Fahredin Shehu has been acknowledged as the 2014 Poet Laureate of the Gold Medal for Poetry by Axlepin Publishing in The Philippines. He was selected for this award from among many globally recognized writers, photographers and painters, all of who had contributed to the betterment of humanity. Other awards through which the author has been recognized include the 'poet of the year' prize by United Nations Asian Federation of Literary Art and Circles, The Six, and ASEAN International Chamber of Commerce (Beijing, China, 2020), 2017 Pulitzer Prize nominee, the Veilero Prize for Poetry (Rome, Italy, 2017), the Naaji Naaman Prize for Poetry (Beirut, Lebanon, 2016), the Poet of the Year Agim Ramadani Prize (Stubëll, Kosovo, 2014), and the Poet of the Year Prize in the Turkish Literary Magazine, IMZA as designated by the Yunus Emre Institute (Prishtina, Kosovo, 2014).

Shehu is a member of the European Academy of Poets and the Poetry Center at Roehampton University in London and holds Doctor Honoris Causa from the Universum Academy in Lugano, Switzerland.

What Others Are Saying . . .

The fragrances of the earth, the fragrances of the past, the fragrance of time that makes human sense . . . Fahredin Shehu inhales all the flavors of existence and does not write, no, but rather exhales the living eons of poetry! His poetry is the spiritualization of air, without which no life is possible! A bottle of Fahredin's age is filling, and miracles are just arriving. What the winds of time do on the outside, the word of the Poet does it on the inside.

Eldar Akhadov, Co-Chairman – the Literary Council of the Assembly of Peoples of Eurasia, Member – PEN International Writing Club, Member – the Union of Writers of Russia, Ukraine and Azerbaijan

♦ ♦ ♦

This is poetry that seemingly rises like a mist, emanating from ancient realms and mystical pathways. Fahredin composes like a bard of old times, weaving verses as if they were musical passages.

Ismail Butera, Musician & Storyteller, USA

♦ ♦ ♦

Fahredin Shehu's poetry elevates the mundane into spiritual realms. The words of his poems are akin to incantations, and he, the Poet, presents himself as an alchemist, creating poetic miracles and wonders from our human experience.

Lena Ruth Stefanovic, Ph.D. in Linguistics, Montenegro

♦ ♦ ♦

There is an elegant clarity to the works of Fahredin Shehu .
. . tactile, olfactory & ocular experiences which many of us
seek to achieve in our work but few achieve. A careful,
gentle voice in love with humanity / the planet and feeling
for its wounds.

Les Wicks, Leading Australian poet & publisher

♦ ♦ ♦

Fahredin Shehu . . . it is the intelligence of the senses, which
is not purely intellectual intelligence that guides and
structures his poetry. Smell, in Proust, could evoke the past,
the "temps perdu". In *Ormus*, the senses also lead us to the
past, to childhood, to the house, that immense world that
lives on in memory. But they also take us further, because
they update love, that love that leads to God. The smell of
wet earth is the sensitive testimony of a paradise, an Eden
that the poet reunites in the Unity that underlies all this
magnificent set of poems.

Alfredo Fressia, Prof. of French letters, poet and literary
critic, Uruguay/ Argentina

♦ ♦ ♦

Fahredin Shehu's Aromatic Memories
(*Ormus* by Fahredin Shehu)

The subtle contextualization of his personal poetry in the
chronotope of the Medieval Orient, in the kingdom of
Ormus/Hormoz, whose etymology refers to the Zoroastrian
deity of Ahura Mazda (Lord of Wisdom) is suggestive of a
hypnotic setting. A retrospection of the soul. A
metempsychotic encounter with the like-minded, an
encounter taken as pure faith, as an outburst of the sacral. A
memory led by the invisible hand of the unconscious. A

poetic laboratory of synesthesia – mixing senses, scents, sounds, colors, tastes, touches.

Fahredin Shehu's poetry is the very touch of that sensitive cocktail that is his poetic language. A reminiscence of the metaphysical quest for oneself by venturing into religious symbolism. Shehu's memory is not only his own. It has absorbed other people's memories as one's own and vice versa. It seeks a world beyond this world, far from ephemeral differences and divisions.

That is why Shehu's poems are meditative, soothing, and their perfume is discrete. The scent of jasmine comes from other times, not from our garden. Its melancholy is pleasant. The past has its own charm – the more scents, sounds, images, tastes and touches it contains, the more powerful it is. That is why it is a palimpsest. Memory turned into word, into verse, into poetry.

Katica Kulavkova, Academic, Ph.D. in Comparative Literature – Sorbonne, poet, Vice President – PEN Global, Skopje, Macedonia

♦ ♦ ♦

Fahredin Shehu's poetry is a glorious Dionysian celebration, a fusion of the senses, revealing the cosmic beauty and giving birth to the Numinous. The reader wanders among colors, sounds and aromas mingled in time and space, combining memory and vision, the mythical and the contemporary. Thus, the golden essence of modern science encounters a "turquoise amphora" and impressions are recorded on an "epitaph of Graphene".

Miriam Neiger-Fleischmann, Literary Scholar (Ph.D.), poet and painter, Jerusalem, Israel

♦ ♦ ♦

The Poems of Fahredin Shehu in *Ormus*

In the beginning, it felt outlandish, and then in slow lento it became familiar. It was the impression I had when I first read the poems of Fahredin Shehu. The feeling of outlandishness was not because I do not know Ormuz, the title of his anthology of poems. It was because I had almost forgotten that this Persian God is well-known throughout the Western world or Europe. He was a famous god, venerated by many people not only in the East, but also in the West, came into the European history together with the emergence of Gnosticism. Both of them had brought the seeds of perennial philosophy to the West as they had to the East.

Such perennial philosophy with Sufistic features is what resonates through Fahredin Shehu's poems in this book. Thus, it was how I began to feel familiar with his poems. His contemplative and meditative poems are beautiful Eastern tones. His poems remind me of Goethe's poems in *Westöstlicher Divan* of two centuries ago.

Goethe's poems were mainly inspired by the romantic Sufi poems of Hafiz, bountiful in spiritual contemplation. In Eastern poetry (such as Chinese, Indian, Persian, Javanese, etc.), there is one reality of poetry: its function as aesthetic mode to express contemplation of one's spiritual experiences. Eastern poets believe that a true poet never indulges in the reality of daily life and he always yearns for her home in the metaphysic realm.

It seems Shehu is a poet like that too. Like Goethe, he seeks the warmth of life in the contrivances of perennial ambience. Such perennial contrivances see that soils in the world are real through the poet's spiritual observance with his meditative experiences. This is my impression when I read Shehu's poems.

Abdul Hadi Wiji Muthari, Professor of Islamic Philosophy and Literature (University Paramadina, Jakarta, Indonesia)

♦ ♦ ♦

In the Light of Ormuz

The title of this book, *Ormus*, is derived from an ancient kingdom and one of most important cities of the East, which controlled trading routes through the Persian Gulf to China, India, and East Africa. The name might be even older, derived from Ashura Mazda, the Persian God of Light. Shehu has long been known for his interest in Sufi mystics. In this pantheistic collection of poems, he becomes truly global, merging the past and the present. Shehu's world is a world between two ears but also a cosmos. He brings eons back to life and to the life of his reader. The sky re-acquires its blueness. He counts tiny little happinesses. He asks for the mercy for confused men. The reader should benefit from his generosity and his power of poetic transformation.

One of the best poets writing in the Albanian language today.

PhD Vladimir Pištalo, Author
Becker College, Worcester, Massachusetts

♦ ♦ ♦

A Masterpiece of Theurgic Power

Ormus for the Soul, Fahredin Shehu's new collection of poems is arriving in a rough and tumble time for poetry. It will have to cut its way to readers through consumerists

"even water is bitter", everything has to be photogenic to be worthy of notice. But Shehu's poetry, being structured to wake up not to be a lullaby, is profoundly forceful. In his poem titled "Integration", he ironically points out that "still none can order a meal with algorithm/ but solely by word." This book is in fact a brave defense of the power of word, that is a defense of poetry against this world of technological supremacy and widely endorsed ideology that empirical evidence is the sole truth and not only of science. Shehu in his poems superbly challenges this established if not dogmatic attitude. He confesses in one of his poems that first he himself was his own challenge and through that experience he has discovered that a great part of this world exists only as sensual evidence and can be measured and expressed only by virtue of Theurgists of Word. Being one of them, he shares with us this book of his sensual evidence as the sole truth. I salute this wonderful theurgic work of complex, lyrically subtle, and imaginatively rich poetry. The heedfully composed stanzas, strophes and verses are fully charged, first with the stream of love of all worlds, then by surmise, blissful inflective and reflective passages, aromatic memories, remnants of a distant past, and all that expressed in magnificently rich language.

As poetical bravado of harmony, rhythm and metaphorical power this book makes a compulsory reading. Believing in the magnanimous extent of poetical capacities, Shehu named this book *Ormus* (elixir) *for the Soul*, provocatively evoking the three Zoroastrian components of life, Ahura (spirit), being the first of them. Yes, our time utterly needs poetry elixirs by the Theurgists of the Word.

I doubt that he who does not pay attention to the theurgic power of the word would be able to comprehend the plenitude of any truth.

Vida Ognjenovic, Professor of Dramaturgy, Global PEN Vice President, Belgrade, Serbia

Other Books

by the

Author

Available at:

www.innerchildpress.com

and other fine bookstores

The author's books listed below have been published by Inner Child Press, AKA Inner Child Press International.

HERENOW (January 7, 2019)

Neon Child (February 14, 2018)

Bonds (December 1, 2016)

Maelstrom. The Four Scrolls of an Illyrian Sage
(October 7, 2014)

Plemora's Dew (April 2, 2012)

HERENOW

FAHREDIN SHEHU

Available at

Inner Child Press.com

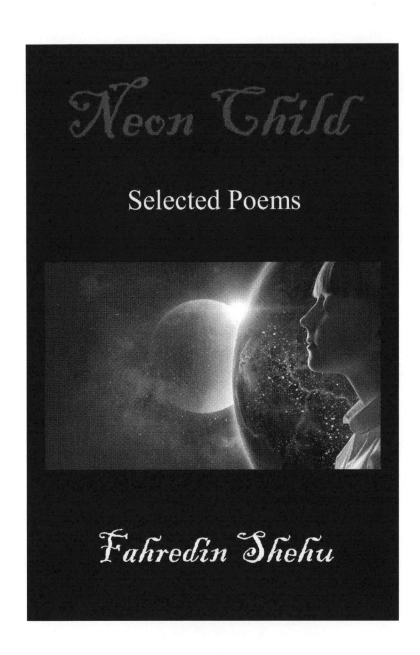

Neon Child

Selected Poems

Fahredin Shehu

Available at

Inner Child Press.com

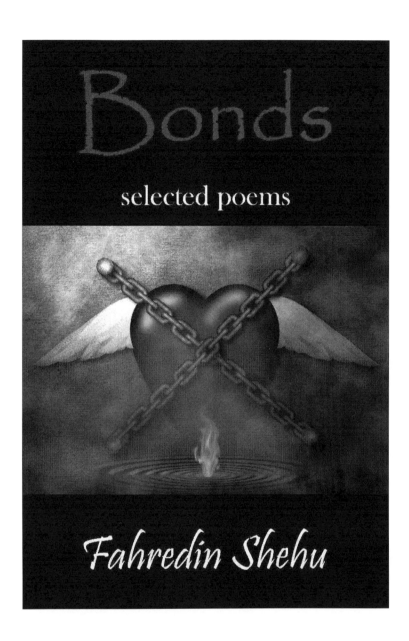

Available at

Inner Child Press.com

Available at

Inner Child Press.com

Pleroma's Dew

the Poetry of

Fahredin Shehu

Available at

Inner Child Press.com

About the Artist

A multimedia artist based in Hamburg, Germany, Shuk Orani has shown his work in Germany and beyond, participating in exhibitions and art fairs throughout European countries and China. As one of the most distinguished painters, he was invited to the Contemporary Art Gallery in Beijing, Louvre Museum in Paris, and Galleria Farini Concept in Italy. Some of his first projects have materialized by demand from luxury boutique hotels and various art studios. He also accommodated boundary transcending, creating artworks for a theatre group.

Orani has also developed some art concepts, some of which have been integrated into various institutions. Predominantly working with oil paintings on canvas, he has had a series of graphic and digital creations as well, sculptures, photographs which often give the viewer the impression of an intimate blink to continuous productivity, as colourful as large scale and perceptibly erotic.

Orani himself is inspired by positive surroundings and the creative capacity of the human being. He believes deeply in art to benefit life with its moving, demanding and satisfying power. His playful manner gives birth to exciting creations, encompassing moods, atmospheres and an inner discourse involving the complex and the simple.

Shuk Orani

Ormus Book Cover

Hamburg, Germany. Transc. In TT TT – Art Project, 2018
Oil on canvas 150 x 200 cm, SO-2018

Upcoming Exhibitions

2020, April – A New York Art Gallery (New York, USA)

2020, May – National Museum of Kosovo (Prishtina, Kosovo)

2020, November – Mark Rothko Museum (Europe & Latvia)

A Selection of Past Exhibitions

2019, December – Atelier Shuk Orani, Personal Exhibition

2019, November – Arte Padova (Italy)

2019, November – Personal Exhibition (Hamburg, Germany)

2019, September – Art Zurich International

2016, August – Moca Museum of Contemporary Art (Beijing)

2015, November – "A Moving Identity" (Cambridge, UK)

2015, December – Galleria Farini (Bologna, Italy)

2015 – Seme, Exposure Photography Award Musée Du Louvre (France)

2015 – Bo Hotel (Hamburg, Germany)

2014 – Exprimere Art Gallery Carapostol (Venice, Italy)

2014 – Arte Padova (Padova, Italy)

2013 – Atelier S. Orani, St. Georg (Hamburg, Germany)

2012 – Swiss Diamond Gallery (Lugano, Switzerland)

2013 – Gallery Z (Vienna, Austria)

2012 – Swiss Diamond Hotel (Prishtina, Kosovo)

2011 – "Ras" National Theater Kosovo (Prishtina, Kosovo)

2009 – Move Sprechwerk Theatre (Hamburg, Germany)

2008 – Gloria Gallery (Hamburg, Germany)

2008 – Art Willa Wedel (Hamburg, Germany)

2007 – BDF Gallery (Hamburg, Germany)

2005 – Palazzo Gallery (Poreč, Croatia)

Long-term Exhibitions

Hotel Palazzo Poreč (Corporate Art) Croatia

Bo Hotel Hamburg (Corporate Art Concept) Ger Rdl Real Estate (Luzern, Switzerland)

Swiss Diamond Hotel (Corporate Art Concept) Integrated Art Concept (Prishtina, Kosovo and Lugano, Switzerland)

Lesna InDesign (Prishtina, Kosovo)

Integradet Art Concept Private Equity and Investments (Germany)

Art Projects, Integrated Art Concepts

2015 – "In2" Oil on Canvas Works Integrated in Engineering Office (Hamburg, Germany)

2013 – "Art & B" Integrated Art Concept, Bo Hotel (Hamburg, Germany)

2012 – "Sdh" Integrated Art Concept, Swiss Diamond Hotel (Prishtina, Kosovo and Lugano, Switzerland)

2011 – "Pca" Integrated Art Concept, Grand Hotel Palazzo (Poreč, Croatia)

2010 – "Ind-L/Pr" Integrated Art Concept, Lesna Interior Design (Prishtina, Kosovo)

Art Projects: Art, Culture and Research

2019-20 – "Transcendence & Transformation", Art Project with Gerd Leins

2017-18 – "8 New Scenes of Qingdao", in collaboration with the Asia Institute within the University of Hamburg & Langyi Museum, Qingdao

2011 – "Ras" Renaissance of Scenic Art in collaboration with the National Ballet of Kosovo

Exhibition, The National Theater of Kosovo

Picture Book and Cultural Concept

2009 – "Move" Project, in collaboration with Cdsh, Contemporary Dance School

Exhibition, Hamburg and Sprechwerk Theater

Picture Book

Inner Child Press

Inner Child Press is a publishing company founded and operated by writers. Our personal publishing experiences provide us an intimate understanding of the sometimes-daunting challenges writers, new and seasoned may face in the business of publishing and marketing their creative "Written Work".

For more information:

Inner Child Press

www.innerchildpress.com

intouch@innerchildpress.com

Inner Child Press International

'building bridges of cultural understanding'

202 Wiltree Court, State College, Pennsylvania 16801

Made in the USA
Coppell, TX
30 August 2021

61469284R00079